AF723759

To My Wife And Family,

For All Their Support Over The Years

(c) 2021 Dr. Stuart P. Wynne
All rights Reserved

No part of this publication may be reproduced or transmitted in any form or by any means without permission of the author.

ISBN: 978-1-8382852-2-7 (print) 978-1-8382852-3-4 (Ebook)

Cataloguing in Publication Data

For more information on this title and others in The Young Explorers' Series visit:

https://www.stuartwynne.co.uk/publications/young-explorers-series/

Wynne, Dr. Stuart P.

The Young Explorers' Guide To Coral Reef Fish

64 pages

The Young Explorers' Guide To

Coral Reef Fish

Book Two Of The Young Explorers' Series

Coral Reefs and Fish

Coral reefs are not only home to many amazingly weird and wonderful creatures, but they are also home to many types of fascinating fish. This is because the coral polyps that make the reef build remarkable structures that fish love to live in. The structures that the coral polyps build can form huge towers and caves that over time create houses in which the fish like to make their home. These formations also attract the food that fish need to eat, and allow a thriving community to grow. This is called an ecosystem, which is very important for the survival of every creature living on the reef.

In The Picture: Shallow coral reefs such as this are home to many types of fish that swim around it and use it as their home. It provides them with protection and also a place to find food and make lots of friends.

Fun Fact:

Coral reefs are extraordinary places and are home to an incredible amount of fish life. In fact these habitats contain the greatest diversity of fish to be found anywhere on the planet! Scientists estimate that there are as many as six to eight thousand species of fish that live in coral reef ecosystems around all of the world's oceans.

Words to Look Up:

Polyp
Structure
Formation
Thrive
Community
Species
Habitat
Diversity

What Is A Fish?

Fish are amazing animals that live in water and breathe using gills instead of lungs. They have lived on our planet for millions of years and are actually our ancestors from before animals evolved arms and legs. Instead, they use fins that allow them to swim around in all directions and find food. Over time these fins have developed some very interesting and strange features that help the fish live in the wonderfully diverse world around them. Sometimes these adaptations make the fish look so strange that it is very hard to know that you are even looking at a fish!

In The Picture: The Bluestriped Grunt in this picture follows the classic fish body plan and fin arrangement. Although its big lips and bright metallic blue body stripes certainly make it stand out from the crowd!

Fun Fact:

It is fascinating to think that all amphibians, reptiles, mammals, and birds alive on the planet today evolved from fish. Scientists think this process began 400 million years ago when certain types of fish (known as tetrapods) began using their fins to shuffle around in shallow muddy areas in search of food. Over time their fins and bodies changed allowing them to live on land all the time.

Words to Look Up:

Ancestor
Evolve
Fin
Feature
Adaptation
Amphibian
Reptile
Mammal

Types of Fish

One of the fun things about fish is that there are so many different kinds! The variety is astounding, from very ordinary and plain looking silver fish that dart through the water, to flat camouflaged fish that lie on rocks barely moving, and huge colourful fish that can grow to the size of a person. Because coral reefs are such diverse habitats the types of fish that live on them are very varied also. It is this incredible diversity and all the wonderful adaptations they have made to help them live on a coral reef that we are going to explore in this book.

In The Picture: Remoras are very strange fish, and spend much of their alone time looking for a sea turtle or shark to attach to. They attach using a large sucker on their heads, and by doing so get a free lift so no longer have to swim!

Fun Fact:

Scientists think that there are over 32,000 species of fish that live in the world's oceans, which is more than all of the mammals, birds, reptiles and amphibians that live on land combined! It is for this reason that it is so important for us to help protect all of these wonderful fish and the amazing habitats in which they live.

Words to Look Up:

Variety
Astound
Ordinary
Camouflage

Fish Babies

Different types of fish reproduce in different ways but the most common method is by laying eggs. Many fish attach their eggs to plants or rocks, while others lay them under the surface of the sand or scatter them directly into the water where they drift around until they hatch. Some species of fish are very dedicated parents and protect the developing eggs that they carefully fix to rocky surfaces. If another fish approaches the eggs the parents sometimes change colour to look more scary as they chase off the potential threat!

In The Picture: Hundreds of tiny eyes look out through their transparent eggs, watching the underwater world go by. Their Sergeant Major Damselfish parents (page 22) defend these eggs vigorously until they hatch.

Fun Fact:

Some fish lovingly place their eggs on rocks and defend them, others let them swim free straight into the sea. One of the most dedicated parents though are the jawfish (page 54), who keep their eggs safely in their mouths until they have hatched. After this the babies still live within the parents mouth until they are old enough to look after themselves, which can be up to eighty days! Thats dedication!

Words to Look Up:

Scatter
Hatch
Protect
Potential
Transparent
Defend
Vigorous
Dedication

Small Silvery Fish

Although many fish on a coral reef are brightly coloured and elaborately decorated, some are quite small and plain. These small fish can form big groups known as 'schools', sparkling when the sun reflects off their shiny skin as they dart around near the reef. These small fish are sometimes babies, and use the reef as a safe place to grow up before they move out into the open ocean to live their adult lives. Sometimes, however, the small silvery fish are actually fully grown adults and live permanently in these groups, swimming over the coral reef as they go about their daily business.

In The Picture: Redear Herring usually travel in large groups with hundreds of others. Here they are zipping over some rocks as they continue their seemingly endless travels over coral reefs and surrounding areas looking for food.

Fun Fact:

The numbers of small silvery fish that are in one school swimming around together can be astounding. Sometimes when threatened by predators they can form what are known as 'bait balls', where they swim around in circles and can number in their millions. By being together in large numbers like this they minimise their chance of capture, a strategy known as 'safety in numbers'.

Words to Look Up:

Elaborate
School of fish
Sparkle
Permanent
Threaten
Minimise
Strategy

Big Silvery Fish: Barracuda

One of the most scary looking fish found living around coral reefs, the barracuda is long and thin, with a sharp pointed face and large fang-like teeth. When barracudas are young they sometimes swim around in small groups, but as they get older they usually prefer to be on their own. These older barracuda drift lazily over the reef, waiting for something of interest to swim past them. This opportunistic strategy saves energy, and when a tasty meal passes by they give a quick flick of their tail and dart forward with incredible speed.

In The Picture: Barracudas are very inquisitive, and will follow divers around underwater and make close approaches from time to time to get a better look. This can feel threatening, but they very rarely get aggressive.

Fun Fact:

Barracudas are one of the most formidable hunters on a coral reef, second only to sharks (page52). They can grow to almost two metres in length and weigh close to 50 kg! Even so, they are capable of astounding speed when attacking their prey and can reach almost 60 kilometres per hour!

Words to Look Up:

Opportunistic
Prey
Inquisitive
Aggressive
Formidable

Big Silvery Fish: Tarpon

Tarpon are one of the biggest silvery fish that can be encountered on coral reefs, and can grow so large that they can sometimes be mistaken for sharks when their large back fin breaches the surface of the water in shallow areas. They have very impressive armoured scales that glint beautifully in sunlight, and are so tough that they have been used by humans in the past as nail files and guitar plectrums! Tarpon are also known for impressive aerobatics and can sometimes jump and flip high out of the water, especially if they are trying to escape from predators.

In The Picture: An Atlantic Tarpon drifting lazily over a coral reef, with its upturned mouth making it look very grumpy indeed! Tarpon may be found drifting in small groups and are known to migrate large distances.

Fun Fact:

Tarpon live in all kinds of habitats, from crystal clear coral reefs to murky estuaries and inlets. They are able to do this as they can fill their swim bladder with air and use it like a primitive lung. This way, they are able to breathe even in cloudy water where other fish would not be able to survive.

Words to Look Up:

Encounter
Breach
Plectrum
Predator
Estuary
Inlet
Swim Bladder
Primitive

Grunts and Snappers

Many species from these two closely related groups of fish start out their life living on seagrass beds or within mangrove tree roots in shallow coastal areas. As they grow larger the young adults move into deeper water and begin their new life as coral reef inhabitants. Both grunts and snappers have the classic fish shape and are usually silver in colour, although some do have bright stripes or blotchy patterns. Grunts are generally smaller than snappers and can form huge schools on reef slopes, under ledges or in ship wrecks. Sometimes snappers even join these groups too!

In The Picture: Two Caesar Grunts cruise together over a coral reef habitat in the Caribbean. In common with most speciess of grunts, these fish like to hang about in groups while they look around for food.

Fun Fact:

Grunts get their name from the strange grunt-like sound they produce when grinding their teeth which are located deep within their throat. Snappers on the other hand get their name from their enlarged front teeth and their habit of snapping their jaws when caught on a fishing line. Watch your fingers!

Words to Look Up:

Seagrass
Mangrove
Coastal
Inhabitant
Blotch
Ledge

Surgeonfish

These oval shaped fish get their name from two extremely sharp spines on the base of their tail fins, reminiscent of a surgeon's scalpel blade. If the surgeonfish is attacked, it flicks its tail fin vigorously from side to side to scare off its attacker. Although surgeonfish are often seen swimming lazily around the reef on their own, they can also form large schools that travel around extensive areas eating algae from the rocks. This keeps corals healthy, because algae grows so fast that it can smother corals if fish and other creatures don't eat it first!

In The Picture: Blue Tang love nothing more than to eat from algae covered rocks. These are the most common species of surgeonfish in the Caribbean, and are in fact one of the most common coral reef fish of all.

Fun Fact:

Surgeonfish are not only one of the most prevalent groups of fish on coral reefs, but they are also very important in terms of how the reef functions. As we learnt above, they love nothing more than to eat algae, and algae is a big problem for baby corals if it is not kept under control. So the more algae surgeonfish eat, the happier the baby corals are!

Words to Look Up:

Extreme
Reminiscent
Scalpel
Extensive
Prevalent

Angelfish and Butterflyfish

Angelfish are among the most beautiful fish that you will see swimming around coral reefs, oval in shape with brightly coloured body patterns and long trailing fins. They are usually seen travelling around in pairs nibbling on sponges (their favourite food), and are known to get very sad and lonely if left alone for too long! Butterflyfish also like to live in pairs, and can remain with the same partner for many years. They look very similar to angelfish, although prefer to eat coral polyps rather than sponges, and are normally smaller in size with less colourful patterns on their bodies.

In The Picture: A Queen Angelfish swimming around a reef area just before dusk. This is one of the Caribbean's most dramatically coloured angelfish, with bright yellow and metallic blue colourations.

Fun Fact:

Butterflyfish may seem to be bad for coral reefs as they eat coral polyps, however this preference is actually a benefit. When scientists study corals they can tell whether a reef is healthy if they see lots of butterflyfish swimming around, as that means there are plenty of healthy corals for them to feed on. This association makes butterflyfish an important "indicator" species of coral reef health.

Words to Look Up:

Trail
Preference
Association
Indicator

Damselfish

Although damselfish are small, they have large personalities and play an important role within the coral reef community. Some are very territorial and tirelessly defend a garden of algae that they carefully grow on rocks near to their homes. They eat this algae, and in doing so help to make space for baby corals to grow. Other species of damselfish are less territorial and spend their time swimming around above the reef in big groups eating plankton and other bits of food that float past.

In The Picture: Threespot Damselfish swim around their territory, ready to chase off intruders at any moment. In this picture, the damselfish was more interested in the camera than scared of it, as it came in for a really close look!

Fun Fact:

Some female damselfish are very choosy when it comes to finding a male partner. The female Bicoloured Damselfish, for example, will spend quite a lot of time examining a male's territory before she decides to stay with him. If the shelter within his territory isn't good enough then she will swim off and look elsewhere for a better looking option.

Words to Look Up:

Personality
Territorial
Tireless
Plankton
Examine
Shelter

Hamlets

At first glance these often inconspicuous fish are very similar to damselfish (page 22) but are in fact more closely related to the groupers (page 26), with large lips and a long down-turned mouth which gives them a characteristically grumpy look. Hamlets range in colour from black all over to brightly patterned with electric blue stripes and spots. They like to eat small crabs, shrimps and the occasional baby fish, and spend most of their time alone, floating quietly a few centimetres above the reef's surface, rarely being seen swimming around in groups or even in pairs.

In The Picture: Barred Hamlets usually spend their time drifting grumpily over a rock or patch of coral rubble. While doing this they hope to spot a tasty shrimp or small crab to have for their dinner.

Fun Fact:

Scientists are unsure if different hamlets with different colourations are separate species or not. This is because although two hamlets who usually choose to breed together look the same as each other, they can also breed with those that are completely different. The babies of these hamlets are a perfect mixture of both parents!

Words to Look Up:

Inconspicuous
Characteristic
Colouration

Groupers

Groupers are some of the chubbiest fish you are likely to meet on a coral reef, with a very large mouth and frequently equally chubby lips! Their mouth turns downwards at the ends which gives them a very grumpy appearance in the same way as with their much smaller hamlet cousins (page 24). In actual fact they are quite shy and swim off and hide if approached rather than get into a fight. Some groupers can grow very large, and most have a varied diet, loving nothing more than to dine on fish, octopus, crabs and shrimps. Yum!

In The Picture: Nassau Groupers can be rather shy, and spend much of their time sitting around on the sea floor or hiding under rocks. These once common Caribbean fish are now unfortunately quite rare due to fishing.

Fun Fact:

Groupers are a type of sea bass, which is a group of fish that comes in a great variety of sizes. The Lantern Bass is one of the smallest, and only grows to a few centimetres in length. Others get very large indeed, with the biggest being the Goliath Grouper which can grow to over two meters in length and weigh as much as a horse!

Words to Look Up:

Chubby
Frequent
Appearance

Parrotfish and Wrasse

One of the most important types of fish which live on coral reefs, parrotfish spend much of their time swimming around and scraping algae off rocks with their strong parrot-like beaks. As we have learnt earlier in this book, it is very important for algae to be kept under control so that baby corals can settle on the rocks and grow. Parrotfish are often brightly coloured, with their patterns and colours changing as they get older. Wrasse, who are closely related to parrotfish, also change colour as they get older but differ by having front teeth rather than a beak. Although wrasse are generally quite small and shaped like torpedoes, some do get very big indeed, with the Humphead Wrasse in the Indo-Pacific growing up to two and a half meters in length!

In The Picture: As with all parrotfish and wrasse, Princess Parrotfish start out life as female. When they grow older and get larger they turn into males, as in this picture, and become the leader of a group of smaller females.

Fun Fact:

When parrotfish scrape algae from rocks and dead coral, they swallow not only algae but also bits of rock too. This rock can't be digested by the fish and so comes out in their poo as sand. It is thought by scientists that 80% of the sand found on beaches near coral reefs is actually made of this material. So without parrotfish there would be very few tropical beaches for tourists to visit!!

Words to Look Up:

Scrape
Torpedo
Indo-Pacific
Digest

Squirrelfish and Soldierfish

Squirrelfish and soldierfish belong to an aptly named group of fish called 'big eyes' that have large dark coloured eyes that are very good for seeing at night. They spend most of the day time lurking under rocky ledges and overhangs, until dark when they leave the protection of thier homes and become more active. During this time they browse the reef looking for small crabs, shrimps and snails to eat. Most squirrelfish and soldierfish are red in colour, with some having golden patches or stripes and others with black markings on their heads.

In The Picture: A Longspined Squirrelfish lurking lazily on a Caribbean coral reef. Most squirrelfish have an elongated rear fin which is one way to distinguish them from their close relatives the soldierfish.

Fun Fact:

Squirrelfish have the amazing ability of communicating with each other by making a vibrating sound from within their body. They use this deep clicking sound to warn off predators or let other squirrelfish know when they are getting too close and entering their territory. These noises join the many other popping and crackling sounds made by small shrimps and other underwater creatures.

Words to Look Up:

Apt
Lurk
Peer
Browse
Consist
Elongate
Distinguish

Gobies and Blennies

Some of the smallest fish that you will find on coral reefs, gobies and blennies are as varied as they are hard to see. Being small, and often blending in extremely well with their background, it is very easy to snorkel around an area and not even know they are there. Although very similar in appearance, it is possible to tell the difference between gobies and blennies as blennies have a long single fin running down their back, whereas in gobies it has been split in two. Both eat a wide variety of food, from filamentous algae to small fish and crabs, and usually spend most of their time sitting motionless on rocks or the surrounding seabed waiting for the next meal to come by.

In The Picture: Sitting peacefully on a sand flat, a Bridled Goby watches the underwater world go past. These little fish sit so still on the seabed, and are so well camouflaged, that it is almost impossible to spot them!

Fun Fact:

As mentioned above, most gobies and blennies spend their time sitting around on rocks. The Sharknose Goby on the other hand drifts around the reef in large groups, looking like a school of baby fish. Only a couple of centimetres in length, its size contrasts with the Giant Goby that can grow to over 30 cm, or the Hairtail Blenny that looks like a snake and can reach over half a metre!

Words to Look Up:

Blend
Snorkel
Filamentous
Contrast

Flatfish

Although most species of flatfish prefer to live on sandy bottoms, a few do live on coral reefs but are usually very hard to spot. This is because many of them are masters of disguise and can change colour to blend perfectly with the surface on which they are lying. One such example is the Peacock Flounder that lives in the Caribbean and has vibrant bright blue circle patterns all over its body resembling the markings on a peacock's tail feathers. It can make these circles disappear if it needs to but can also flash them suddenly if startled, which helps to scare off predators.

In The Picture: Peacock Flounders spend hours resting on rocks, blending in perfectly with their surroundings. With only their two strange eyes and oddly placed mouth showing, these fish only move if threatened or to grab a meal.

Fun Fact:

Flatfish are able to lie flat on the seabed due to a clever evolutionary trick that they have developed over time. When they are young, flatfish look like normal fish with one eye on each side of the head. As they grow older though one of these eyes gradually moves across its face until it is on the other side of the head!

Words to Look Up:

Disguise
Vibrant
Resemble
Startle
Gradual

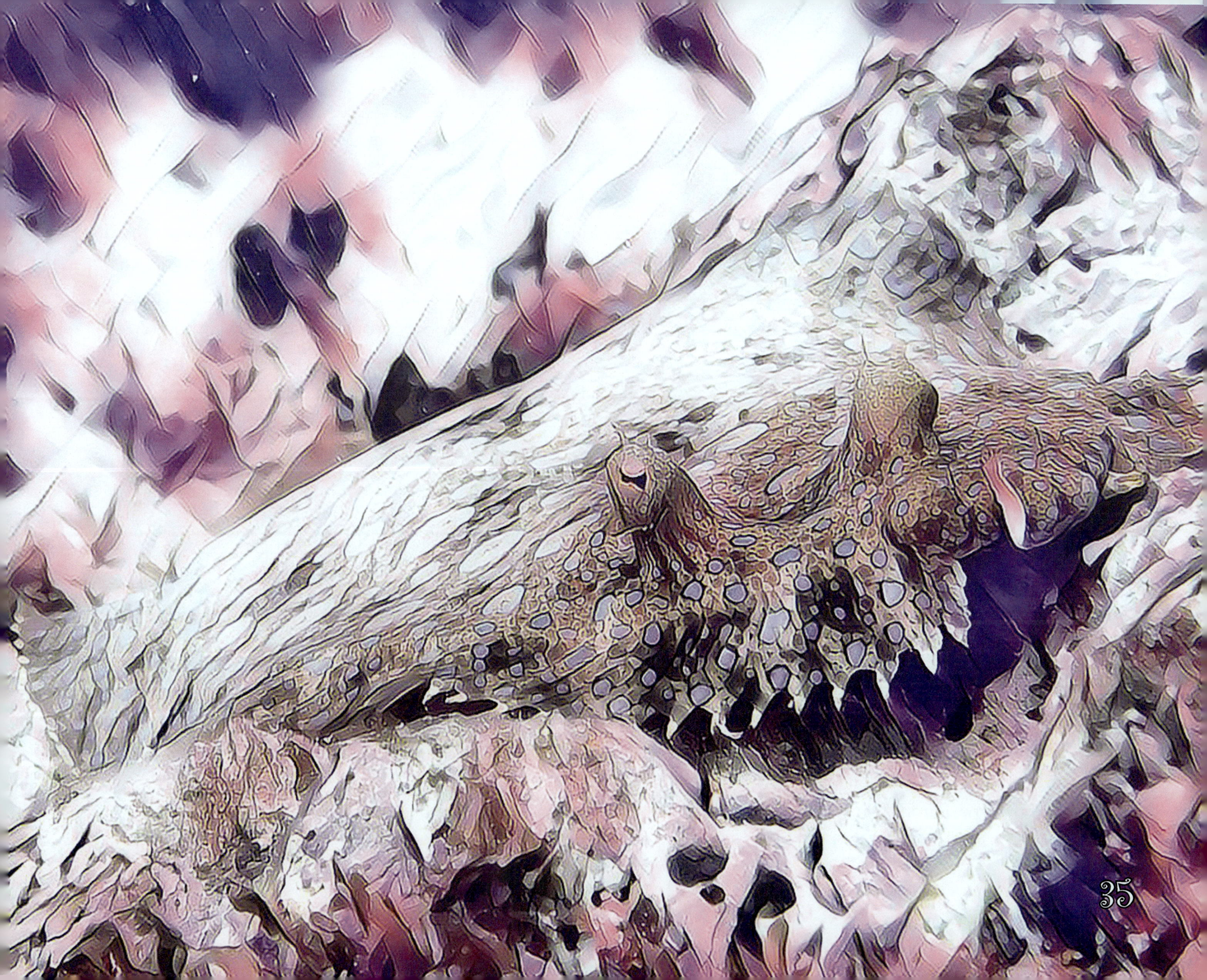

Lionfish and Scorpionfish

Lionfish and scorpionfish are closely related, although they look and behave very differently from each other. One of the most beautiful types of fish to be encountered on a coral reef, lionfish have very long, elaborate striped fins that splay out like fingers around its body. It uses these to herd small fish and corner them close to rocks before capturing them. Scopionfish are very different in appearance, usually with only small knobbly protrusions over their body which act as perfect camouflage while sitting motionless on rocks waiting for unsuspecting prey to pass by. Lionfish and scorpionfish both have venomous spines on the end of their fins that can give a very powerful and painful sting if touched......an extremely useful defense from predators!

In The Picture: A Red Lionfish on a Caribbean reef surrounded by soft corals and sea fans. Although incredibly beautiful, these fish have become quite a menace over recent years because of their voracious appetite for local fish.

Fun Fact:

Lionfish are probably one of the most successful coral reef invaders of all time. They are native to the Indo-Pacific region but were accidentally released into the Caribbean basin in the early 1990s. Since then they have spread throughout the entire area and are now one of the most common predatory fish around......not good news for the local fish population!

Words to Look Up:

Splay
Protrusion
Unsuspecting
Venomous

Lizardfish

As their name suggests, lizardfish have a very reptilian face that usually looks very grumpy and menacing. In fact, they are quite reclusive fish and spend most of their time lying on rocks or the seabed, blending in and hoping not to be spotted as they wait for passing prey. Lizardfish have slender cylindrical bodies and their lizard-like mouths are full of sharp teeth. Interestingly, they even have teeth on their tongue, which must make it even more unpleasant if one decides it wants you for its supper! Luckily for us, their preferred food are small fish and invertebrates. Phew!

In The Picture: A Sand Diver lying lazily on some rocks waiting for its next meal to pass by. You can see from its face that it doesn't look very happy to have been spotted......although in actual fact they always look this way!

Fun Fact:

Lizardfish that live on coral reefs are relatively small, and do not usually grow much larger than 40 cm in length. A close relative however, known as the Deepsea Lizardfish, can grow considerably larger, the biggest of which was recorded to be almost a metre in length and weighed nearly 7 kg!

Words to Look Up:

Reptilian
Menace
Reclusive
Slender
Cylindrical
Considerable

Trumpetfish

With a long thin body and trumpet-shaped head and mouth, trumpetfish are among the most peculiar types of fish likely to be seen on a coral reef. They spend much of their time floating lazily around the reef or hiding close to soft corals and seaweed. Despite this, trumpetfish are actually quite aggressive predators and use their stealth ability to closely approach small fish from behind. They then rapidly open their long mouths, creating a strong suction force which sucks their prey straight into the mouth, a little bit like an underwater vacuum cleaner!

In The Picture: When they are not hunting, trumpetfish spend much of their time hanging out among soft corals and seaweed, hiding from predators. They use their long shape and striped body patterns as camouflage.

Fun Fact:

Trumpetfish are closely related to pipefish and seahorses. Seahorses are fascinating fish and unique because the father gives birth to the young rather than the mother. He is given the eggs by the mother and keeps them safe in a special pouch until they are ready to hatch. Once hatched the tiny little seahorses swim out of the pouch and begin their adventure into the underwater world.

Words to Look Up:

Peculiar
Stealth
Ability
Suction
Vacuum cleaner
Pouch

Porcupinefish and Pufferfish

Porcupinefish are a very bizarre type of coral reef fish indeed. When they are swimming around the reef normally they do not look very different from other fish, apart from being slightly chubby and covered in flattened spines. However, if they are threatened by a predator they have the ability to inflate into a ball and erect all their spines. This behaviour will startle the potential predator and their puffed up size combined with the erect spines would make them very nasty to eat! However, as an unfortunate side-effect it can take a few hours for a porcupinefish to deflate, during which time they are less mobile and more susceptible to harm. Pufferfish are closely related and very similar to porcupinefish although their spines are often less prominent.

In The Picture: This Spiny Pufferfish was captured accidentally in a fishing net and puffed up to show off its spines. After being taken out of the net it was returned to the water and later went back to its business unharmed.

Fun Fact:

Even if a predator gobbles up a porcupinefish or pufferfish before it inflates, it won't enjoy the experience. Most contain a toxin that makes them foul tasting and potentially deadly if eaten. The toxin is also deadly to humans, with enough poison in one fish to kill 30 adult humans, and there is no known antidote. Despite this, in Japan pufferfish are considered a delicacy for the brave!

Words to Look Up:

Erect
Inflate/deflate
Susceptible
Prominent
Antidote
Toxin
Delicacy

Boxfish

A close relative of porcupinefish (page 42), boxfish are so called because they have a hard box-like body made up of hexagonal interlocking plates. If looked upon from the front they are triangular in shape with small fins that allow the fish a high degree of manoeuverability. Boxfish are one of the cutest types of fish that live on coral reefs, with large eyes and a small, pouting, chubby-lipped mouth which they use to pluck small shrimps and worms off the surrounding rocks. There are a number of different types of boxfish, from the unassuming trunkfish to the aptly named cowfish which have two horns on their head, resembling those of a bull. Unlike porcupinefish, boxfish can not inflate their body, instead relying on their hard body and camouflage for protection.

In The Picture: A Honeycomb Cowfish swimming across a coral reef in the Caribbean. Its name comes from the hexagonal pattern over its body that resembles honeycombs, like those found in bee hives.

Fun Fact:

One of the characteristics that boxfish share with their porcupinefish relatives is a toxin that they produce as protection from predators. Unlike the porcupinefish however, boxfish secrete this toxin through their skin when stressed, rather than having it present within their body all the time. As the toxin cannot be produced after death, it means boxfish are far safer for us to eat.

Words to Look Up:

Hexagonal
Interlock
Manoeuverable
Pout
Unassume
Secrete

Triggerfish

Sometimes referred to as 'leatherjackets' due to their thick skin, many triggerfish are majestic looking fish, with beautiful trailing fins and bright vibrant colours. Their tough skin is especially useful as some love nothing more than eating very spiny sea urchins, which they dive into head first, crushing their shells with their sharp powerful mouth. There is a lot of diversity among the triggerfish, from the darkly coloured Black Durgeons who cruise around the water column in large groups, to reclusive Sargassum Triggerfish that like to live in deeper water and swim around the rocks on the seabed looking for food. Triggerfish get their name from a lockable 'trigger' just behind their head that they can erect to make it really hard for a predator to fit them in their mouths!

In The Picture: A Queen Triggerfish who has just set its sights on a tasty sea urchin and is about to dive in and take its first bite. Luckily it has very thick skin, so this spiky meal shouldn't be too much of a problem to eat!

Fun Fact:

Some species of triggerfish can be very territorial and will aggressively defend their nests during their reproductive season. The aggression of the Titan Triggerfish is so well known that divers who venture underwater will move away very quickly if they see one approaching. Their bite is so powerful that it has been known to take big chunks out of divers flippers leaving them in tatters!

Words to Look Up:

Majestic
Lockable
Reproductive
Venture
Flipper
Tatter

Filefish

Filefish are closely related to triggerfish (page 46), and are very similar in appearance, but the main difference between them is that their 'trigger' is not lockable and looks more like a carpenter's file. Some types of filefish, are very small and spend their lives hiding among plants such as seagrass, whereas others are much larger and more colourful, proudly swimming around the coral reef looking for food. One of the most unusual types is known as the Scrawled Filefish and lives in the Caribbean. It is very long and slender with a pointed snout, and vibrant irregular metallic blue lines and spots all over its body that can flash and change colour a little bit like disco lights. Party time!

In The Picture: One of the smallest filefish there is, the Fringed Filefish grows to only a couple of centimetres in length. Some of its relatives can be much larger, and may reach over half a metre!

Fun Fact:

Filefish have small mouths, but inside are a number of strong sharp teeth which they use to break off pieces of coral to eat. Scientists have recently discovered that filefish camouflage themselves not only by changing their body colours, but also by using chemicals within the corals they eat. These chemicals make the fish smell like coral and so help with their clever disguise!

Words to Look Up:

Movable
Metallic
Chemical

Eels

These long thin fish at first glance look more like a snake than anything else, but on making a closer inspection their long continuous fin is visible. This fin starts behind the head and stretches down its back, encircling the tail and extending halfway along the underside of its body. Eels live in both rivers and the sea all over the world. Those that are found on coral reefs are voracious predators of other fish, usually hiding in small rocky holes, striking out suddenly if a tasty looking meal passes by. They have very sharp backward pointing teeth that mean once grabbed, prey stand very little chance of escape!

In The Picture: A Spotted Moray Eel pokes its head out from a rocky hole, opening and closing its mouth in a very scary manner. However, they do this to move water through their gills, rather than it being an aggressive threat.

Fun Fact:

Of all the types of eel that live on or around coral reefs, morays are probably the most impressive and vicious looking. The largest is the Giant Moray Eel which lives in the Indo-Pacific region and can grow to over three metres in length. On the other end of the scale, the Hawaiian Dwarf Moray Eel is one of the smallest and rarely grows larger than 25 cm. That's quite a difference!

Words to Look Up:

Glance
Inspection
Encircle
Intricate
Voracious

Sharks and Rays

Sharks are very large aggressive looking fish found in all ocean habitats around the world, including those where corals live. They are usually grey and white in colour with big mouths filled with very sharp teeth, which they use to eat all sorts of prey including fish, sea turtles and marine mammals such as dolphins. Rays are closely related to sharks but are very different in both appearance and behaviour. They have a flattened body with wide side fins that look like wings, which some use to cruise lazily around sifting plankton out of the water for food. Others lie quietly on sand patches and dig up food with their noses. Rays can be beautifully patterned with bright spots and other markings or, like Sharks, can be grey in colour with white tummies.

In The Picture: A Reef Shark swimming near the surface over the top of a shallow coral reef area. This is the most common shark associated with coral reefs in the Caribbean, but happily is not considered dangerous to swimmers!

Fun Fact:

Although sharks and rays are fish, they are very different from the other types talked about in this book. Instead of bones, their body structure is made of cartilage, which is a much lighter and more flexible material. They also do not have 'swim bladders', which other fish have to help them to stay buoyant. Due to this, if sharks or rays stop swimming they sink!

Words to Look Up:

Sift
Cartilage
Buoyant

Other Coral Reef Fish

There are many other types of fish that live on coral reefs other than those featured in this book, with the diversity being truly amazing. For example, Flying Gurnards have hard heads and fabulous brightly patterned side fins that they can spread out like wings to startle predators. Needlefish are very long and pointy and swim around quickly just under the surface of the ocean darting around for food. Spotted Drums have vivid black and white stripes and, as babies, have long trailing fins that are many times longer than their body. Other types of fish to look up and learn about include seahorses, goatfish, and tilefish. How many others can you find out about? Make a list and write down all the fascinating facts that you can discover about them!

In The Picture: Jawfish are both great parents (see fun fact on page 8) and very tidy, spending a lot of their time moving small rocks and coral fragments around which they use to line the entrance of their burrows.

Fun Fact:

Clownfish spend much of their lives living among sea anemone tentacles, the stings of which do not harm them. The anemone also benefits from this living arrangement as it is thought that the bright colours of the clownfish help to lure in smaller fish that the anemone then catches and eats. A relationship between two animals where both benefit from each other is known as symbiosis.

Words to Look Up:

Tentacle
Arrangement
Lure
Relationship
Symbiosis

Fish Conservation

Coral reef fish populations are threatened around the world by human activities such as over-fishing and pollution, which can lead to climate change. This harms them because changing sea temperatures can damage the coral that these fish rely on for food and places to live. We can all do our bit to help reduce our impact on the environment by recycling our rubbish and using less gas and electricity in our homes. Doing this means less pollution for our planet and so less damage to the plants and animals that live on it. This way future generations will also be able to enjoy the wonderful world we live in.

In The Picture: A huge school of French Grunts (page 16) sheltering near a large coral covered rock. Also in the picture are striped Sergeant Major Damselfish (page 22) and Blue Tang Surgeonfish (page 18). Can you see them all?

(Not So) Fun Fact:

It was first noticed that coral reefs were in trouble during the 1970s when a disease swept through huge areas of the Caribbean killing a great many corals. Scientists now think that if human activities do not change up to 90% of corals will die over the next twenty years as a result of pollution and warming oceans. This will be disastrous for coral reef fish and people who rely on them for food.

Words to Look Up:

Conservation
Population
Over-fishing
Climate Change
Environment
Generation
Disastrous

Index Of Words To Look Up:

Index Of Words To Look Up:

Look Out For Book Three Of The Young Explorers' Series:

The Young Explorers' Guide

To Sea Turtles

www.ingramcontent.com/pod-product-compliance
Ingram Content Group UK Ltd
Pitfield, Milton Keynes, MK11 3LW, UK
UKRC031203030826
14089UKWH00031B/245

* 9 7 8 1 8 3 8 2 8 5 2 2 7 *